# healing with
# herbs

## a concise guide
## to natural herbal
## remedies for
## everyday ailments

**Jessica Houdret**

HERMES
HOUSE

Publisher: Joanna Lorenz
Production Controller: Joanna King

Publisher's Note:
The Reader should not regard the recommendations, ideas and techniques
expressed and described in this book as substitutes for the advice of a
qualified medical practitioner or other qualified professional.
Any use to which the recommendations, ideas and techniques
are put is at the reader's sole discretion and risk.

Printed in Hong Kong/China

3 5 7 9 10 8 6 4

# contents

# introduction

Herbal medicine is holistic in its approach: it aims to treat the underlying causes of illness as well as the actual symptoms. Herbs have always played a key role in the physical and emotional health and wellbeing of people, and many well-known herbs have a direct medicinal action, with antiseptic, antibacterial qualities. Taken as a regular part of the diet, sprinkled over food or taken as herbal teas and decoctions, herbs can help to ward off illness, promote health and cure minor ailments. Others herbs have uplifting scents that promote a feeling of renewed energy when used externally in ointments, inhalations, essential oils, compresses and poultices.

# The benefits of herbs

 **The definition of what constitutes a herb has broadened over the centuries. Nowadays the term "herb" includes any plant whose roots, stem, leaves, flowers or fruit is used to flavour food, as medicine or for scent.**

Most people are familiar with herbs that are commonly used in cooking, such as basil, bay, chives, mint, oregano, parsley, sage and thyme. But taking into account the broader definition of the term "herb", one can include plants such as aloe vera, spices such as ginger, flowers such as marigolds and roses, and fruits such as lemons and rose-hips.

As well as adding aroma and delicious flavour to food, culinary herbs have some nutritional value, often containing appreciable amounts of vitamins, minerals and trace elements. Adding herbs to your food on a daily basis actively promotes good health. Many herbs have excellent digestive qualities, helping the body to process and eliminate oily, fatty or gas-producing foods. But adding a generous sprinkling of fresh or dried herbs to your food is not the only way to benefit from these versatile plants.

▼ HERBS WILL GROW IN THE SMALLEST OF SPACES, SO LONG AS THEY ARE NURTURED.

### Herbal Medicine

Many herbs have a therapeutic and medicinal value and can be taken in a variety of forms to prevent and cure illness and to promote health. Taken internally they can be made into herbal teas, decoctions, tinctures and inhalations. Externally they can be applied as compresses, poultices, ointments, creams or infused oils. Herbs add their aroma to bath water for a therapeutic soak and essential oils distilled from the flowers can be used for a massage.

Best of all, herbs are widely available and grow in the smallest of spaces ensuring a continual year-round supply for everyone.

▲ FRESH HERBS AID DIGESTION AS WELL AS ADDING VITAL FLAVOUR TO FOOD.

▼ WARMING SPICES SUCH AS GINGER AND CINNAMON ADD HEAT TO FOOD AND DRINKS, HELPING TO WARD OFF COLDS AND CHILLS.

# Herbal teas

One of the easiest ways to benefit from the properties of a herb is to drink it as a tea. Taken regularly, herbal teas can make a significant contribution to wellbeing with their soothing, refreshing, and invigorating qualities.

▲ THYME TEA IS GOOD FOR STOMACH CHILLS AND CHEST INFECTIONS.

Herbal infusions make wonderfully refreshing drinks and can be drunk as caffeine-free alternatives to ordinary tea and coffee. Herb teas, or tisanes, as they are sometimes known, are an acquired taste, so if you are unsure whether or not you like them, persist a little longer. The flavour of most can be sweetened with honey, a licorice stick, slices of fresh ginger or a squeeze of fresh lemon.

Herbal tisanes contain general health-giving properties and act as a refreshing tonic when taken regularly. Many commercial brands are available, but the taste is inferior to those made from fresh or

## CAUTION

Herbs are powerful and can be harmful if taken in excess. Do not make teas stronger or drink them more frequently than recommended. Seek medical advice before taking herbal remedies when pregnant.

home-dried garden herbs. Using herbs from your garden also ensures that the maximum benefit will be extracted. Since many herbs have a specific medicinal quality, you could grow those that suit your needs for a year-round supply.

Herbal teas can be taken to help ward off colds and flu, to aid digestion, promote sleep, to relieve headaches, anxiety and stress, even to promote energy. Drink a cupful of the appropriate tea no more than three times a day. Teas can be stored for up to 24 hours in the refrigerator.

**1** Allow 30ml/2 tbsp fresh or 15ml/ 1 tbsp dried herb to each 600ml/ 1 pint/2½ cups water. For a single cup (250ml/8fl oz), use two small sprigs of fresh or 5ml/1 tsp dried herb. Wash fresh herbs first.

**2** Put the herbs into a warmed pot. Pour on boiling water. Replace the lid to prevent vapour dissipation.

**3** Leave to brew for three or four minutes, then strain the tea into a cup for a refreshing drink.

# Herbal tea remedies

You don't necessarily have to feel ill to enjoy the benefits of a herbal brew, since many can be enjoyed as a refreshing drink at any time of day. However if you do have specific symptoms, the combinations below will certainly help.

## Coughs and colds

| | |
|---|---|
| PURPLE SAGE AND THYME | USE 5ML/1 TSP OF EACH FRESH PER CUP. ADD 1.5ML/ ¼ TSP CAYENNE PEPPER FOR A MORE POWERFUL EFFECT. |
| PEPPERMINT, ELDERFLOWER, CHAMOMILE AND LAVENDER | USE 2.5ML/½ TSP OF THE FIRST THREE, WITH A PINCH OF LAVENDER, PER CUPFUL OF WATER. |
| HOREHOUND | USE FRESH OR DRIED, AND SWEETEN WITH HONEY. |
| HYSSOP | USE FRESH OR DRIED, AND SWEETEN WITH HONEY OR MIX WITH ORANGE JUICE. |
| THYME | USE 5ML/1 TSP DRIED OR 10ML/2 TSP FRESH PER CUP. |

## Digestive troubles

| | |
|---|---|
| CHAMOMILE | USE 5ML/1 TSP OF DRIED FLOWERS PER CUP. |
| PEPPERMINT AND LEMON BALM | USE FRESH HERBS IN EQUAL MEASURE AFTER A MEAL. |
| DILL | CAN BE GIVEN TO BABIES AND YOUNG CHILDREN. ALLOW 2.5ML/½ TSP LIGHTLY CRUSHED DILL SEED TO A CUP OF WATER AND BOIL FOR TEN MINUTES. STRAIN AND LEAVE TO COOL. |
| FENNEL SEED | CRUSH THE SEEDS AND SIMMER IN AN ENAMEL PAN FOR TEN MINUTES BEFORE STRAINING. CARAWAY SEEDS CAN BE PREPARED IN THE SAME WAY. |
| CINNAMON | INFUSE A CINNAMON STICK IN BOILING WATER FOR THREE OR FOUR MINUTES. LEAVE TO COOL, THEN CHILL. |

## Tonics and pick-me-ups

| | |
|---|---|
| STINGING NETTLES | CHOP A SMALL HANDFUL OF YOUNG, FRESH LEAVES AND INFUSE IN 600ML/1 PINT/2½ CUPS BOILING WATER BEFORE STRAINING. |
| SPEARMINT | USE 15ML/1 TBSP CHOPPED FRESH LEAVES PER CUP AND SWEETEN TO TASTE. |
| BASIL | ADD THREE OR FOUR LEAVES PER CUP. |

## Early morning wakeners

| | |
|---|---|
| LEMON VERBENA | USE FRESH OR DRIED LEAVES TO WAKE UP YOUR SYSTEM. |
| PEPPERMINT | USE ONE SPRIG OF FRESH HERBS PER CUPFUL. |
| BERGAMOT | USE FRESH FLOWERS FOR AN "EARL GREY" TASTE. |

## Disturbed sleep

| | |
|---|---|
| CHAMOMILE | MAKE WITH 5ML/1 TSP DRIED CHAMOMILE TO A CUP AND ADD A PINCH OF LAVENDER FOR EXTRA RELAXATION. |
| LIMEFLOWER AND ELDERFLOWER | ADD A DASH OF GRATED NUTMEG AND SWEETEN WITH HONEY OR FLAVOUR WITH LEMON JUICE. |
| VALERIAN | USE 10ML/2 TSP DRIED AND SHREDDED ROOT TO A CUP OF WATER AND SIMMER FOR 20 MINUTES IN AN ENAMEL PAN WITH A LID. LET IT COOL, THEN STRAIN AND REHEAT IT. |

## Headaches, anxiety, and depression

| | |
|---|---|
| ROSEMARY | USE ONE OR TWO SMALL SPRIGS PER PERSON. |
| LEMON BALM | USE FRESH LEAVES. |
| ST JOHN'S WORT | USE FRESH OR DRIED LEAVES AND FLOWERS. |
| PASSIONFLOWER, VALERIAN AND MOTHERWORT | USE 5ML/1 TSP DRIED VALERIAN AND MOTHERWORT AND ADD TO IT 2.5ML/½TSP OF PASSIONFLOWER. |

▼ CHAMOMILE TEA IS SOOTHING AND CALMING.

# Herbal decoctions

Infusing herbs in boiling water is not enough to extract the constituents from roots or bark, such as valerian or licorice. Harder plant material needs to be boiled, and the resulting liquid is called a decoction.

**1** To make a decoction, wash the roots thoroughly.

**2** Chop the root into small pieces.

**3** Add 5ml/1 tsp of the root or bark to a pan of cold water. Leave it to soak for ten minutes, bring it to the boil, allow to simmer for 15 minutes.

**4** Strain off the liquid and allow to cool slightly. Decoctions can be kept for 24 hours in the refrigerator. They can be drunk hot or cold.

## TIP
Always use a stainless steel, glass or enamel pan, when preparing herbal remedies.

### Herbal decoction recipes
**CHILBLAINS** SIMMER 15G/½OZ CHOPPED GINGER ROOT IN 750ML/ 1¼ PINTS/3 CUPS OF WATER UNTIL THE LIQUID REDUCES TO 600ML/ 1 PINT/2½ CUPS. STRAIN AND STORE IN THE REFRIGERATOR. TAKE 5–20ML/ 1–4 TSP THREE TIMES A DAY.
**GALL BLADDER PROBLEMS** SIMMER 50G/2OZ CLEAN, CHOPPED DANDELION ROOT IN WATER. STRAIN THROUGH A SIEVE AND STORE IN THE REFRIGERATOR FOR UP TO THREE DAYS. TAKE IN DOSES OF 5–20ML/1–4 TSP THREE TIMES A DAY.

# Herbal tinctures

A tincture is a medicinal extract in a solution of alcohol and water. Take it diluted in a little water or fruit juice, but do not exceed 5ml/1 tsp, three or four times a day. Alternatively, use it externally, by adding it to liniments and compresses.

**1** Place 115g/4oz dried herbs or 300g/11oz fresh herbs in a jar.

**2** Add 250ml/8fl oz/1 cup vodka and 250ml/8fl oz/1 cup water.

**3** Leave to steep for two weeks, in a sunny place. Strain. Store in a dark, cool place for up to 18 months.

## Herbal tincture remedies

**HEADACHES AND DEPRESSION**
USE LAVENDER IN THE QUANTITIES GIVEN ABOVE. TAKE DILUTED, OR ADD TO A COMPRESS.

**MOUTH ULCERS AND INFLAMED GUMS**
USE RASPBERRY LEAF IN THE QUANTITIES GIVEN ABOVE. DILUTE IN AN EQUAL QUANTITY OF WARM WATER AND USE AS A MOUTHWASH.

**RHEUMATISM** USE JUNIPER IN THE QUANTITIES GIVEN ABOVE AND ADD IT TO A LINIMENT FOR ACHING JOINTS.

**COLDS** USE DRIED ELDERFLOWER IN THE QUANTITIES GIVEN. TAKE DILUTED.

# Essential oils

**Essential herb oils are most commonly associated with aromatherapy, but they have a number of beneficial uses. Choosing to use these oils can be a quick and convenient option if you don't have a ready supply of herbs to hand.**

▲ IT TAKES VERY LITTLE ESSENTIAL OIL TO PERFUME A ROOM.

## USING A BURNER

Burning essential oils perfumes the air and creates an inner sense of wellbeing. You will need a special burner (available from chemists and herbalists) which consists of a shallow bowl over a small chamber containing a night light. Pour 15ml/1 tbsp of cold water into the bowl, then add a few drops of oil, light the night-light and sit back and relax. As the water evaporates you will need to top it up. Never leave a burning flame unattended for any length of time.

## INHALATION

Essential oil can be used as an inhalation. Fill a bowl with steaming water and add a few drops of essential oil. Lean over the bowl with a clean towel covering your head and the bowl and breathe in through the nostrils.

## IN THE BATH

Relax in a scented bath and enjoy the soothing benefits of an essential oil. Dilute no more than ten drops in a vegetable oil carrier, then add the mixture to your bath.

### Essential oil remedies

**ATHLETE'S FOOT** ADD TEA TREE OIL TO A FOOT BATH.

**BROKEN VEINS** ADD NEROLI OR ROSE OIL TO A COMPRESS.

**ECZEMA** ADD A FEW DROPS OF BERGAMOT, GERANIUM, JUNIPER OR SANDALWOOD OIL TO A WARM BATH.

**NEURALGIA** ADD BLACK PEPPER OIL TO A WARM BATH OR A COMPRESS.

**SCARS** TREAT WITH FRANKINCENSE OIL.

**WARTS AND VERRUCAS** ADD LEMON OR TEA TREE OIL TO A COMPRESS.

# Cold infused herbal oils

 Use these cold-infused oils in massage, as bath oils or for conditioning the hair and the skin. When a herb is steeped in oil, the aroma of the herb, as well as its essential oils, permeate the liquid.

**1** Fill a glass storage jar with the cleaned flowers or leaves of dried herbs – choose from rosemary, lavender, St John's wort, chamomile or marjoram.

**2** Pour in a light vegetable oil to cover the herbs – try sunflower or grapeseed oil.

**3** Allow the jar to stand on a sunny windowsill for a month for the flavours to steep. Give it a shake every day.

**4** Strain the ingredients. For a stronger infusion, renew the herbs every two weeks. Pour into dark bottles and keep for eight weeks.

# Herbal ointments

An ointment contains oils or fats, but not water, and is useful to form a protective layer over the skin. For a natural method use a vegetable oil such as sweet almond or sunflower, with beeswax. This is easy to make at home.

**1** Place the beeswax and the oil in a glass bowl over a pan of water. Bring the water to the boil and simmer until the wax has melted into the oil. Remove from the heat.

**2** Stir continually as the oil/wax mixture cools and stiffens. Add your choice of essential oils and stir into the mixture.

**3** Pour or spoon into small, clean ointment jars, seal and store. Make small quantities and use it as soon as it is made.

▲ APPLY OINTMENTS SPARINGLY AND COVER THE TREATED AREA TO PROTECT FROM DIRT.

# Herbal creams

Making an organic cream is very similar to making an ointment, again using beeswax. Keep the cream in a cool place away from direct sunlight, and preferably in a dark glass or china pot. It should not be kept indefinitely.

## BASIC RECIPE

25g/1oz beeswax
25ml/1½ tbsp water
120ml/4fl oz/½ cup vegetable
   oil such as almond, safflower,
   sesame or grapeseed oil
20–30 drops essential oil, or
   10 drops if the ointment is
   for sensitive skin

**1** Melt the oil and beeswax as for the herbal ointment. Add water to the melted wax/oil mixture, drop by drop, stirring all the time until the cream thickens and cools.

**2** Add the essential oils and gently stir them into the cream.

### Herbal cream and ointment recipes

PROBLEM SKIN ADD ROSE OIL.

MATURE SKIN ADD JASMINE OIL.

FOR HEALING CUTS AND GRAZES ADD MARIGOLD OIL.

FOR HEALING ACNE ADD SANDALWOOD OIL TO THE CREAM.

TO NOURISH, CLEANSE AND SOOTHE THE SKIN MELT 50G/2OZ WHITE BEESWAX WITH 115G/4OZ ALMOND OIL. IN A SEPARATE BOWL DISSOLVE 2.5ML/½TSP BORAX IN 50ML/2FL OZ/¼ CUP OF ROSEWATER. SLOWLY POUR THE BORAX MIXTURE INTO THE OIL AND WAX, WHISKING UNTIL IT COOLS. WHEN IT THICKENS POUR INTO GLASS POTS.

**3** Carefully pour or spoon the cream into small, clean dark-coloured ointment jars. Seal and then store in the refrigerator.

# Herbal poultices

Mashed herbs form the basis of a poultice. Its main purpose is to aid the healing of bruises, sprains and sores. Poultices are applied direct to the skin, either hot or cold. Hot poultices help sprains, while cold help inflammations.

**1** Snip a handful of herb leaves into a dish. Cover with boiling water and mash to a pulp with a spoon.

▼ A POULTICE IS AN INSTANT METHOD OF USING HERBS.

**2** Leave to cool slightly, then spread the pulp directly on to the affected area. Cover with a piece of gauze and a bandage. Leave in place for several hours.

## Herbal poultice recipes

SUNBURN LIGHTLY CRUSH THE LEAVES AND STEMS OF ANGELICA AND APPLY DIRECT TO THE SKIN.

GRAZES AND SCRAPES MASH SAGE LEAVES. APPLY DIRECT TO THE SKIN.

ACHING JOINTS AND MUSCLES MIX EQUAL AMOUNTS OF THE FRESH OR DRIED LEAVES OF MARJORAM AND ANGELICA AND APPLY TO THE SKIN.

STINGS AND BITES MIX OATMEAL TO A PASTE WITH AN INFUSION OF COMFREY OR MARIGOLD. LEAVE TO COOL. APPLY TO THE SKIN.

# Herbal compresses

A compress is a length of fabric that is applied to the skin after it has been dipped into a herbal infusion. Compresses are gentle remedies that can be used for many different complaints from headaches to period pains.

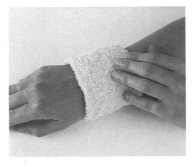

**1** Put fresh or dried herbs into a clean bowl. Pour over boiling water. Leave to stand for one hour, then strain the liquid. Allow to cool, then mix in any essential oil. Soak a length of cotton in the infusion and wring out lightly.

**2** Position on the affected area and hold in place with a bandage.

▾ COMPRESSES CAN BE USED EFFECTIVELY ON ANY PART OF THE BODY.

### Herbal compress recipes

TIRED EYES  USE A SMALL HANDFUL OF CHAMOMILE FLOWERS TO MAKE AN INFUSION. DIP MUSLIN IN THE COOLED LIQUID AND APPLY TO THE CLOSED EYELIDS FOR 20 MINUTES.

BRUISES  MAKE AN INFUSION USING 25G/1OZ FRESH WORMWOOD OR 15G/½OZ DRIED WITH 500ML/17FL OZ/2¼ CUPS BOILING WATER. LEAVE FOR 30 MINUTES THEN STRAIN. APPLY COOL.

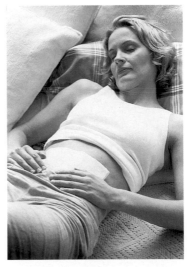

# the herbal
# medicine chest

The recipes that follow make use of the roots, bark, leaves, stems and flowers of many different herbs. Be aware before you begin that herbs are a potent source of medicine, containing essential oils and potentially therapeutic properties that can be harmful if misused, or used in larger quantities than specified in each recipe. Pregnant women should avoid all kinds of herbal remedies unless under professional supervision. Always use herbs from a reliable source, and if you are unsure what the herb is, then do not use it.

# Coughs and colds

The common cold affects most people at some point in the year. And since there are over 200 strains of cold virus, it is not surprising that a cure has not been found. Herbal treatments can help to relieve many of the symptoms.

GARLIC COLD AND FLU SYRUP
With antiseptic and antibacterial qualities, garlic is ideal for a cold.

*INGREDIENTS*

 1 head garlic, crushed
 300ml/½ pint/1¼ cups water
 juice of ½ lemon
 30ml/2 tbsp honey

**1** Bring the garlic and water to the boil. Simmer gently for 20 minutes.

**2** Add the lemon juice and honey and simmer for two minutes. Allow to cool, then strain into a clean, dark bottle with an airtight lid. Take 10–15ml/2–3 tsp three times a day. Keep chilled for up to three weeks.

EVERYDAY ROSE-HIP TEA
Rose-hips are high in vitamin C and help to ward off colds.

*INGREDIENTS – MAKES ABOUT 6 CUPS*

 45ml/3 tbsp rose-hips
 1.5 litres/2½ pints/6¼ cups
 filtered or bottled still water

**1** Top and tail the rose-hips. Cover them in tap water for 24 hours. Strain and discard the water.

**2** Bring the filtered water to the boil. Add the rose-hips. Simmer for about 30 minutes. Strain and serve, adding honey to sweeten, if liked.

LAVENDER AND EUCALYPTUS VAPOUR
The fresh and uplifting scents of lavender and eucalyptus clear the chest and nasal passage. Rub on the chest before bedtime.

*INGREDIENTS*

*50g/2oz petroleum jelly*
*15ml/1 tbsp dried lavender*
*6 drops eucalyptus essential oil*
*4 drops lavender essential oil*

**1** Melt the jelly in a bowl over a pan of simmering water. Stir in the lavender and heat for 30 minutes.

**2** Strain the liquid through muslin. Cool, then add the oils. Pour into a clean jar and leave until set.

▲ THIS VAPOUR RUB CAN ALSO BE INHALED. MELT A SMALL QUANTITY IN A BOWL OF STEAMING WATER. LEAN OVER THE BOWL, WITH A TOWEL OVER YOUR HEAD AND INHALE. KEEP THE CREAM REFRIGERATED.

## Herbal cough remedies

TRY A WARM INFUSION OF ONE OR A MIXTURE OF THE FOLLOWING:
**COLTSFOOT** – PARTICULARLY GOOD FOR IRRITATING, SPASMODIC COUGHS
**HYSSOP** – A CALMING AND RELAXING EXPECTORANT
**MARSHMALLOW** – FOR A HARSH, DRY, PAINFUL COUGH
**THYME** – POWERFULLY ANTISEPTIC, THIS RELIEVES A HARSH, DRY AND PAINFUL COUGH
**HOREHOUND** – AN EXPECTORANT, FREEING UP MUCUS AND HELPING IT TO BE REMOVED.

## Herbal cold remedies

TAKE AN INFUSION OF EQUAL AMOUNTS OF PEPPERMINT, ELDERFLOWER AND YARROW JUST BEFORE BED TO INDUCE A SWEAT. YOU CAN ALSO ADD:
**CAYENNE PEPPER** – USE 1.5ML/¼ TSP OF THE POWDER TO STIMULATE THE SYSTEM. CAYENNE ADDS INSTANT HEAT AND WILL MAKE YOU SWEAT.
**CINNAMON** – BREAK A CINNAMON STICK INTO THE HERBS FOR A GENTLE, WARMING AND SWEAT-INDUCING EFFECT.
**GINGER** – GRATE A SMALL PIECE OF FRESH ROOT GINGER INTO THE MIXTURE FOR EXTRA HEAT.

# Sore throats

**Often a sore throat goes hand-in-hand with the symptoms of a cough or cold. Sometimes sore throats can be caused by air conditioning in office buildings. Gargling with an infusion of herbs or sipping herbal teas can ease the discomfort.**

ALLIUM STEAM INHALATION

Garlic has antiseptic properties that will ease a sore throat.

**1** Put two unpeeled garlic cloves in a heatproof bowl containing 1 litre/ 1¾ pints/4 cups of steaming water.

**2** Lean over the bowl, cover your head with a towel and inhale the garlic steam for several minutes.

▶ TAKE A CUP OF GINGER AND LEMON DECOCTION TWICE A DAY.

GINGER AND LEMON DECOCTION

Warming ginger has expectorant properties and lemon is rich in vitamin C. Both soothe a sore throat.

*INGREDIENTS*

*115g/4oz piece of fresh root
ginger, peeled and sliced
juice and rind of 1 lemon
pinch of cayenne pepper
600ml/1 pint/2½ cups water*

**1** Put the ginger and lemon rind in a pan with the pepper and water. Bring to the boil, cover and simmer for 20 minutes. Remove from the heat and add the lemon juice.

▲ THE CONEFLOWER, *ECHINACEA ANGUSTIFOLIA* OR *E. PURPUREA*, BOOSTS THE IMMUNE SYSTEM AND MAY BE TAKEN IN TABLET FORM OR AS A TINCTURE.

## SOOTHING LARYNGITIS

Laryngitis is an acute inflammation of the larynx or vocal chords, leading to a sore throat, hoarseness and even loss of voice. Local treatment is by gargle or cold infusions. The best herbs to use are sage, thyme, agrimony or raspberry leaf. Leave a small handful of leaves to infuse in boiling water, then strain and allow to cool. For a soothing effect, add marshmallow.

### Tonsillitis remedies

MAKE AN INFUSION OF AGRIMONY, LICORICE, SAGE, OR THYME TO GARGLE WITH. A TINCTURE OF MYRRH IS ALSO GOOD.

## THYME AND SAGE GARGLE

This recipe will relieve sore throats, mouth ulcers, gum disease, laryngitis and tonsillitis.

*INGREDIENTS*

*15g/½oz fresh sage and thyme, or hyssop and horehound*
*600ml/1 pint/2½ cups boiling water*
*30ml/2 tbsp cider vinegar*
*10ml/2 tsp honey*
*5ml/1 tsp cayenne pepper*

**1** Put your choice of herbs into a bowl, pour in the boiling water, cover and leave for 30 minutes. Strain the liquid.

**2** Stir in the vinegar, honey and cayenne. Gargle or swallow 10ml/ 2 tsp at a time, twice a day.

▼ SAGE AND THYME ARE BOTH ANTISEPTIC.

# Blocked sinuses

Inhaling steam scented with aromatic herbs relieves the congestion of a cold or blocked sinuses and can remove the headaches which are often a symptom of the problem. You could put essential oils on your pillow and in your bath too.

ESSENTIAL OIL INHALANT
Add 5 drops of eucalyptus, 2 drops of camphor and 1 drop of citronella essential oils to 600ml/1 pint/ 2½ cups of boiling water and inhale.

FRESH HERB INHALANT
To relieve blocked sinuses, immerse fresh herbs and spices in steaming water and breathe in the vapours. Choose from: eucalyptus leaves, basil, cayenne pepper, cinnamon stick, hyssop, juniper berries and foliage, lavender, lemon balm, mint, rosemary, sage, thyme.

1 Put a large handful of your chosen herbs in a bowl and pour in about 1 litre/1¾ pints/4 cups of boiling water. Lean over the bowl, covering both it and your head with a towel. Inhale deeply.

# Earache

**Earaches most often develop through an infection, often following a cold or sinusitis. They should not be neglected – infections can spread through into the middle or even inner ear with potentially serious complications.**

If earache is associated with catarrh, this should be treated too. Earache in children needs to be treated quickly as an infection in the middle ear can be both painful and damaging. Seek medical help if earache worsens or persists.

Do not put anything into the ear, unless it has been examined by a doctor to check that the eardrum has not been perforated.

▲ Burning lavender and chamomile oil will bring relief to earache sufferers.

▲ Chamomile contains the anti-inflammatory chemical azulene which is useful for treating conditions such as earache, acne, insect bites and allergies.

## Earache remedies

**Chamomile** – make a hot compress, or an infusion. Apply to the outside of the ear with cotton wool (swab).

**Garlic** – eaten with food, or if the eardrum is not perforated, crush 1 clove of garlic into 5ml/1 tsp of olive oil; warm it to blood temperature and gently insert a few drops into the ear. This is an excellent antibiotic.

# Winter blues

The transition from autumn to winter is not always easy, particularly when the nights draw in and the warm weather disappears. To help you to adapt to this changing time, there are plenty of uplifting herbal remedies.

ROSEMARY TONIC WINE

This pungent and aromatic herb has a long tradition of use as a tonic herb with a reputation for lifting the spirits.

*INGREDIENTS*

*handful of fresh rosemary*
*    leaves*
*2 small cinnamon sticks*
*5 cloves*
*5ml/1 tsp ground ginger*
*grating of nutmeg*
*bottle of claret or other good*
*    quality red wine*

**1** Put the rosemary, cinnamon and cloves into a jar and crush using a pestle to release their essential oils. Add the ginger and nutmeg to the mixture.

**2** Add the wine, seal the jar and leave in a cool place for ten days. Strain into a sterilized bottle and seal with an airtight stopper.

▶ St John's wort.

## Winter brightener

The old herbalists thought that the appearance of a plant held a clue to its healing action – St John's wort, for example, resembles the sun, thrives in sunlight and is an anti-depressant.

*INGREDIENTS*

*10ml/2 tsp dried St John's wort*
*5ml/1 tsp dried rosemary*
*250ml/8fl oz/1 cup boiling water*

**1** Combine the herbs and steep in boiling water for ten minutes.

**2** Strain and drink twice a day throughout the winter, but not for more than two weeks at a time.

## Alcohol-free tonic

Add 600ml/1 pint/2½ cups of boiling water to 2.5ml/½ tsp each of oats, vervain, St John's wort and borage. Flavour with peppermint or licorice. Allow to steep for ten minutes, then strain. Drink two cups of the tea warm, each day, for no more than three weeks.

## Restorative tea

Mix equal parts of St John's wort, porridge oats and damiana. Put 10ml/2 tsp of the mixture in a teapot with 600ml/1 pint/2½ cups boiling water. Steep for ten minutes then strain. Drink a cup twice a day.

◀ FRESH OR HOME-DRIED HERBS MAKE THE BEST HERBAL TEAS, BUT IF YOU DON'T HAVE ACCESS TO A SUPPLY, SHOP BOUGHT HERBAL TEA BAGS CAN BE SUBSTITUTED.

# Headaches

**The majority of headaches are caused by nasal congestion or sinusitis, eyestrain, fatigue or tension. They can also be caused by stress or worries, with muscle spasms in the neck and upper back leading to head pains.**

WOOD BETONY AND LAVENDER TEA
These herbs soothe the nerves and are helpful for tension headaches. You could try chamomile, or lime blossom tea to relieve a headache.

*INGREDIENTS*

*2.5ml/½ tsp dried wood betony*
*2.5ml/½ tsp dried lavender*
*200ml/7fl oz/scant cup boiling water*

**1** Put herbs into a cup and leave to steep in the boiling water for up to ten minutes.

**2** Strain and drink twice a day.

Caution: Do not take more than 5ml/1 tsp betony per day.

▲ LAVENDER HAS A DELICIOUS, UPLIFTING SCENT. USE IT TO PERFUME A BATH.
▼ RUB LAVENDER OR ROSEMARY OIL INTO YOUR TEMPLES TO RELIEVE A HEADACHE.

### Herbal headache remedies

HANG A MUSLIN BAG OF FRESH OR DRIED HERBS UNDER THE TAP WHEN YOU RUN A BATH. MAKE A LAVENDER OR ROSEMARY COMPRESS BY SOAKING SOFT COTTON FABRIC IN A LAVENDER OR ROSEMARY INFUSION AND WRINGING IT OUT SLIGHTLY BEFORE APPLYING IT TO YOUR FOREHEAD.

# Hangovers

**Most hangover symptoms – headache, nausea, fuzzy head and depression – are connected with the liver being unable to perform many of its crucial functions. Bitter herbs stimulate the liver. Do not take vervain if you have liver disease.**

MORNING-AFTER TEA

Vervain is bitter and lavender aids digestion; both lift the spirits.

*INGREDIENTS*

*5ml/1 tsp dried vervain*

*2.5ml/½ tsp lavender flowers*

*600ml/1 pint/2½ cups water*

**1** Bring the water to the boil and add the herbs. Cover the pan of boiling water to retain the volatile oils, and remove from the heat.

**2** Allow to steep for ten minutes. Strain and sweeten with a little honey. Sip a cup of this tea slowly.

▲ IF YOU HAVE A HANGOVER, DRINK PLENTY OF WATER TO FLUSH THROUGH YOUR BODY, AND TAKE EXTRA VITAMIN C. A CUP OF BOILING WATER WITH A SLICE OF LEMON IN IT, OR FRESHLY SQUEEZED LEMON JUICE WILL GIVE THE LIVER A BOOST.

▼ HERBAL TEAS PROMOTE WELLBEING.

# Migraines

**These are more than a severe headache. They generally involve acute pains, often over one eye, and perhaps disturbed vision or flashing lights. There may also be nausea or vomiting and sensitivity to bright lights.**

NECK MASSAGE FOR MIGRAINE
Use rosemary essential oil to massage your neck. Keep your arms relaxed while massaging.

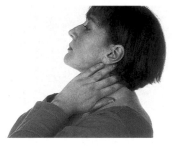

**1** For stiff, aching neck muscles massage the neck with firm circular movements.

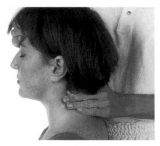

**2** Ideally have someone else massage your neck for you. They can support your head while massaging.

## Herbal tea remedies to relieve migraines

CHOOSE FROM CHAMOMILE OR ROSEMARY, ACCORDING TO YOUR TYPE OF MIGRAINE. MAKE AN INFUSION OR TEA WITH THE CHOSEN HERB AND SIP IT THROUGHOUT THE DAY.

**CHAMOMILE** IS GOOD FOR A DULL, THROBBING HEADACHE WITH A FEELING OF QUEASINESS – ADD A LITTLE GINGER TO RELIEVE MORE SEVERE NAUSEA.

**FEVERFEW** RELIEVES THE FEELING OF A TIGHT BAND AROUND THE HEAD. IT IS ALSO AVAILABLE IN TABLET FORM.

**ROSEMARY** HELPS WHERE STRESS IS A TRIGGER FOR MIGRAINES AND WHERE LOCAL WARMTH GIVES RELIEF.

▲ FEVERFEW LEAVES ARE VERY BITTER. THE BEST WAY TO TAKE THEM IS SANDWICHED BETWEEN TWO SLICES OF BREAD.

# Tense muscles

When we are anxious, we raise our shoulders and contract our back muscles. The effort of maintaining our muscles in this way is tiring. Tight neck muscles can also prevent adequate blood flow to the head and so bring on a headache.

COLD-INFUSED LAVENDER OIL

This recipe is easy to make and very versatile. You could make marjoram or rosemary oils in the same way.

*INGREDIENTS*

*dried lavender heads*
*clear vegetable oil*

**1** Fill a jar with lavender heads and cover completely with oil. Replace the lid. Allow to steep in a sunny place for a month. Shake daily.

**2** Strain and bottle. Massage into stiff muscles or add to your bath to encourage relaxation.

TIP
• Do not use concentrated essential oil on your skin, dilute it by adding 2 drops of oil to 20ml/4 tsp of grapeseed or almond oil.

▼ IF YOU SPEND A LOT OF TIME STANDING OR SITTING IN THE SAME POSITION YOU NEED TO KEEP STRETCHING AND RELAXING YOUR LIMBS.

# Insomnia

**It is important to distinguish between habitual sleeplessness and temporary insomnia caused by worry. Do not become obsessed with trying to get a certain amount of sleep; not everyone needs eight hours.**

LAVENDER TINCTURE

Store tinctures in dark bottles in a cool place for best results.

*INGREDIENTS*

*15g/½oz dried lavender*
*250ml/8fl oz/1 cup vodka, made up to 300ml/½ pint/1¼ cups with water*

**1** Put the lavender into a glass jar and pour in the vodka and water. Put a lid on the jar and leave in a cool, dark place for ten days (no longer), shaking occasionally. The tincture turns dark purple.

**2** Strain off the lavender through a muslin before pouring into a sterilized glass bottle. Seal with a cork.

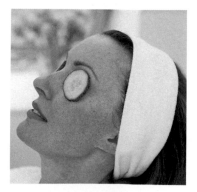

▲ TRY FILLING A MUSLIN BAG WITH LAVENDER AND PUT IT UNDER THE BATH TAP WHEN FILLING THE BATH. ADD LIGHTED CANDLES TO HELP CREATE A RELAXING ATMOSPHERE.

▼ TAKE TIME TO UNWIND BEFORE YOU GO TO BED. LISTEN TO SOOTHING MUSIC AND PAMPER YOURSELF WITH A CUCUMBER FACIAL.

## Herbal insomnia remedies

MAKE THE HERBS LISTED BELOW INTO TINCTURES OR USE THE DRIED HERB TUCKED UNDER YOUR PILLOW.

| | |
|---|---|
| CHAMOMILE | LAVENDER |
| HYSSOP | LEMON BALM |
| LIME BLOSSOM | VIOLET |
| PASSIONFLOWER | VALERIAN |

# Anxiety

**Some degree of anxiety in everyday life is inevitable, since it is a natural mechanism for dealing with stress. But when the degree of anxiety is out of proportion to the problem, trouble arises.**

Anxiety induces many of the following symptoms in most people:
• Constant feelings of tension
• Sweating
• Palpitations
• Irritability
• Hyper-ventilating
• Lack of sleep
However, there are many herbal remedies to help you cope.

CALMING ANXIETY TEA
Choose from chamomile, lemon balm, lime blossom, skullcap or valerian and use 5ml/1tsp dried herb or one sprig of fresh to one cup of boiling water.

▲ LICORICE CALMS THE STOMACH, HELPING TO ALLEVIATE THE SYMPTOMS OF ANXIETY SUCH AS STOMACH CHURNING.

## Herbal remedies for anxiety
WILD OATS, VERVAIN, WOOD BETONY AND SKULLCAP (USE 2.5ML/½ TSP EACH PER CUP OF WATER), ST JOHN'S WORT, LICORICE, OR BORAGE FLOWERS TAKEN AS A TEA.
THE FOLLOWING ESSENTIAL OILS MAY BE USEFUL: BENZOIN, CHAMOMILE, EUCALYPTUS OR LAVENDER.

### Remedies to reduce sweating
VALERIAN OR MOTHERWORT TAKEN AS A TEA.

### Remedies to induce sleep
PASSIONFLOWER TAKEN AS A TEA.

◄ PASSIONFLOWER HAS SEDATIVE PAIN-RELIEVING PROPERTIES.

# Stress

**Stress in itself is not harmful and can in fact be motivating. But when the amount of stress is too much for our system to cope with, then it can cause other more harmful medical conditions.**

STRESS-BUSTER TEA

Choose relaxing infusions from herbs such as lavender, lime blossom, lemon balm and valerian. A mixture of vervain, rosemary and betony (no more than 2.5ml/½ tsp per cup) are a tonic for exhaustion.

*INGREDIENTS*
*30ml/2 tbsp fresh or 15ml/*
*1 tbsp dried herb*
*600ml/1 pint/2½ cups boiling*
*water*

**1** Put the herbs and water in a teapot. Steep for ten minutes.

▲ EXERCISE HELPS TO REMOVE TENSION AND CHANGES THE FOCUS OF YOUR ATTENTION.

SYMPTOMS OF STRESS
• Constantly on edge and on the verge of tears.
• Difficulty in concentrating.
• Always tired, even after a night's sleep, and unable to relax or unwind – even if not working.
• Feelings of being unable to cope with life.
• Poor appetite or else nibbling without hunger.
• No sense of fun or enjoyment.
• Mistrustful of everybody.
• Problems in relationships, no interest in sex.
• Always fidgeting or biting nails or chewing hair.

▲ AVOID CAFFEINE WHEN YOU ARE STRESSED. CHOOSE HEALTHY HERBAL TEAS INSTEAD.

# Indigestion

**An excess of very rich food or alcohol can cause symptoms of indigestion such as bloating, acidity and heartburn. A herbal remedy that relaxes the nervous system will calm muscles in the digestive tract and reduce spasm in the gut.**

CALMING TEA

Hops, lemon balm and chamomile all have sedative, calming qualities that will ease digestion and calm the stomach muscles.

*INGREDIENTS*

5ml/1 tsp lemon balm
5ml/1 tsp hops
5ml/1 tsp chamomile
600ml/1 pint/2½ cups boiling water

**1** Put the herbs into a warmed cafetière (press pot) or teapot and fill with the boiling water. Allow to steep for no longer than ten minutes, then strain into a teacup.

**2** Drink one cup no more than three times a day after a meal. Take as a medication, not everyday.

▲ FENNEL TEA WILL HELP TO RELIEVE INDIGESTION. CRUSH THE SEEDS FIRST.

TO RELIEVE WIND AND COLIC

In a pan boil 5ml/1 tsp each of fennel seeds and cramp bark with about 300ml/½ pint/1¼ cups water. Add 5ml/1 tsp dried peppermint. Allow to steep for ten minutes then strain and drink.

▼ A GENEROUS SPRINKLING OF HERBS WILL AID THE DIGESTION OF FOOD.

## Herbal teas for indigestion

| | |
|---|---|
| CHAMOMILE | FENNEL |
| HOPS | LEMON BALM |
| LICORICE | MEADOWSWEET |
| PEPPERMINT | SLIPPERY ELM |

# Acidity and heartburn

**Bouts of acidity and heartburn tend to occur after consuming rich foods or eating too quickly, and can be a symptom of indigestion. If the condition is temporary, make teas from the suggested herbs. Seek help if the problem persists.**

MEADOWSWEET TINCTURE
This herb is a traditional remedy for heartburn, gastric ulcers and excess acidity.

*INGREDIENTS*
*115g/4oz dried, or 300g/11oz freshly picked meadowsweet flowers*
*250ml/8fl oz/1 cup vodka*
*250ml/8fl oz/1 cup water*

**1** Place the herb flowers in a jar. Pour in the vodka and water.

**2** Put a tight-fitting lid on the jar and leave to steep for a month, preferably on a sunny windowsill. Gently shake the jar.

▲ PEPPERMINT TEA IS A GOOD TEA TO TAKE FOR INDIGESTION AND ACIDITY.

**3** Strain and store the tincture in a dark glass bottle (it will keep for up to 18 months).

**4** Take 5ml/1 tsp, three times a day, diluted in a little water or fruit juice.

◀ GROW MEADOWSWEET IN YOUR GARDEN AND ADD THE LEAVES TO STEWS OR SOUPS IF YOU ARE PRONE TO HEARTBURN.

### Herbal teas for acidity and heartburn

| | |
|---|---|
| CHAMOMILE | LEMON BALM |
| MEADOWSWEET | PEPPERMINT |

# Abscesses

**An abscess is a localized, inflamed swelling containing pus which can develop externally on the skin or internally in the mouth or other mucous membranes – the latter should be treated by a medical professional.**

HOT MARSHMALLOW POULTICE

A poultice made of marshmallow to heal an inflammation is one of the earliest recorded uses for a herb.

*INGREDIENTS*
*    2 handfuls fresh marshmallow*
*      leaves or 15ml/1 tbsp*
*      powdered marshmallow root*
*    250ml/8fl oz/1 cup of boiling*
*      water or about 45ml/3 tbsp of*
*      hot water*
*    olive or almond oil*

**1** Pour the boiling water over the leaves in a bowl. If you are using powdered root, mix it with a little hot water to make a paste.

**2** Apply a little oil to the skin in the affected area first, so that the poultice does not stick and burn the skin. Place the leaves or the paste on the abscess and cover with clean gauze or strips of cotton, lint or muslin.

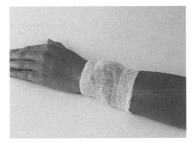

**3** Hold in position with tape or a safety pin. You can keep the poultice on for several hours but may need to replace the contents of it every couple of hours. It is likely to feel damp and uncomfortable to begin with.

# Bites and stings

**Summer brings a host of insects such as bees, wasps and hornets that can sting. In any situation where a bite or sting affects the mouth or throat, or if there are signs of an allergic reaction, get medical help immediately.**

MARIGOLD INFUSION

Only the pot marigold *Calendula officinalis* has a medicinal value, so make sure you choose the right one when picking your flowers.

*INGREDIENTS*

> *heatproof bowl*
> *1 litre/1¾ pints/4 cups boiling water*
> *20 marigold flower-heads*

**1** Warm the bowl. Place the flowers in the bowl. Pour over the water. Cover with a dish towel. Leave to stand for ten minutes.

**2** Strain the liquid into a bottle. Apply the infusion as a skin lotion or on a cold compress to ease the pain of a bite or sting.

REMOVING A STING

Some stings, for instance those of bees, result in the sting being left behind in the skin. This should be carefully removed before applying any ointments or herbal preparations to the affected area. Try flicking it out with a sharp knife or using tweezers if your hand is not so steady. Take care, however, not to squeeze the poison sac and thereby send more toxin into the puncture hole.

## Bite and sting remedies

COMPRESS – WORMWOOD, WITCH HAZEL, CHAMOMILE, ELDERFLOWER, RED CLOVER, MARIGOLD, LAVENDER, LEMON BALM, PLANTAIN, YELLOW DOCK.
FRESH HERBS – ALOE VERA, HOUSELEEK, LEMON BALM, BASIL, DOCK LEAF, ONION.
OINTMENT – CHICKWEED, MARIGOLD.
POULTICE – CARROT (FOR SUNBURN), OATMEAL.
TINCTURE – ST JOHN'S WORT.

◀ MARIGOLD IS USED IN SKIN CREAMS TO SOOTHE AND HEAL.

# Cuts, grazes and bruises

Before treating any cuts, grazes and bruises, make sure that the affected area is properly cleaned with water and a clean cloth to remove any dirt. An ointment will help to draw out dirt that is deeply embedded in the skin.

COMFREY BRUISE OINTMENT

Apply this ointment to varicose veins, bruises and inflamed muscles.

*INGREDIENTS*

   *200g/7oz petroleum jelly or*
    *paraffin wax*
   *25g/1oz fresh comfrey leaves*

**1** Put the petroleum jelly in a bowl. Set it over a pan of boiling water, add the chopped comfrey leaves and stir well. Heat over gently simmering water for about one hour.

**2** Strain the mixture through muslin secured to the rim of a bowl with an elastic band. Pour the liquid into a clean glass jar, before it has chance to set.

## Herbal remedies for cuts and grazes

COMPRESS – WITCH HAZEL (THOUGH NOT ON BROKEN SKIN).
OINTMENT  MARIGOLD, COMFREY.
POULTICE – SAGE.
TINCTURE – MARIGOLD, MYRRH, YARROW.

## Herbal remedies for bruises

COMPRESS – WITCH HAZEL, COMFREY, WORMWOOD.
ESSENTIAL OILS – LAVENDER.
OINTMENT – HOUSELEEK, YARROW.
POULTICE – COMFREY.

▲ USE COMFREY SPARINGLY AND NEVER TAKE IT INTERNALLY.

# Burns and sunburn

**Severe burns require medical assistance. The immediate treatment is to apply cold water for up to ten minutes to reduce the heat. With sunburn, be sure to avoid further exposure to the sun until all the symptoms have cleared.**

AFTER SUN SOOTHING OIL

A cooling oil for burnt skin.

*INGREDIENTS*

  *5 drops rose essential oil*
  *5 drops chamomile essential oil*
  *45ml/3 tbsp grapeseed oil*
  *45ml/3 tbsp virgin olive oil*
  *15ml/1 tbsp wheatgerm oil*

**1** Combine the oils in a small bowl. Massage gently into the burn.

MARIGOLD OINTMENT FOR BURNS

This ointment moisturizes and soothes the skin.

*INGREDIENTS*

  *200g/7oz petroleum jelly*
  *about 25g/1oz marigold flower heads, roughly chopped*

**1** Put the petroleum jelly in a bowl. Set it over a pan of boiling water, add the marigolds and stir. Heat over simmering water for one hour.

**2** Strain the mixture through muslin secured to the rim of a jug with an elastic band. Pour the liquid immediately into a clean glass jar, before it has a chance to set. Leave to cool then refrigerate.

## TIPS
• Aloe vera gel is an excellent first-aid treatment for burns. Break open a leaf and spread the gel directly on to the burn.
• You could also try infusions of elderflower, rose, chamomile, lavender, and tea tree.

# Halitosis and mouth ulcers

Bad breath can result from several things such as an upset stomach, or teeth that need cleaning. For an instant breath freshener chew fresh parsley after a meal. Mouth ulcers are an indication of being run down. Herbs can help both.

SAGE AND SALT TOOTHPOWDER

This toothpaste replacement will clean your teeth and keep your breath fresh.

*INGREDIENTS*
    25g/1oz sage leaves
    60ml/4 tbsp sea salt

1 Shred the sage leaves into an ovenproof dish using scissors.

2 Mix in the salt, grinding it into the leaves with a pestle. Bake in a very low oven for about one hour until crisp.

3 Pound the baked ingredients until reduced to powder. Use in place of toothpaste on a damp toothbrush.

MYRRH AND SAGE MOUTH ULCER RINSE
*Sage has antiseptic qualities and is a good herb for mouth complaints.*
*INGREDIENTS*
    *15ml/1tbsp dried sage*
    *100ml/½ pint/1¼ cups boiling water*
    *10ml/2 tsp tincture of myrrh*

1 Put the sage leaves in a bowl. Pour the boiling water over. Leave to stand for 20 minutes, strain and mix in the myrrh. Allow to cool. Use to rinse your mouth.

---

### Herbal mouth ulcer tinctures

| MYRHH | MARIGOLD |
|---|---|
| RASPBERRY LEAF | SAGE |
| THYME | |

### Herbal teeth cleansers

RUB TEETH WITH FRESH SAGE LEAVES.

# Acne and spots

 Congested skin pores cause acne and spots. During teenage years, acne is caused by increasing levels of hormones, which cause the skin's glands to overproduce sebum, (the natural oily skin lubricant), so blocking the pores.

CHAMOMILE STEAM FACIAL

The heat of this treatment relaxes and opens the pores in the skin and boosts blood circulation in the face. Close the pores afterwards by dabbing with a cooled skin toner or using a face mask.

*INGREDIENTS*

*40g/1½ oz fresh or 15g/½ oz dried chamomile flowers or mint, marjoram, marigolds or rose petals*
*600ml/1 pint/2½ cups boiling water*

1 Make an infusion of the fresh or dried flowers in boiling water. Leave to stand for 30 minutes then strain.

2 Reheat the infusion and pour it into a large bowl.

3 Cover both your head and the bowl with a towel and inhale for about 30 seconds. Repeat two or three times. Close the pores with a skin toner.

▾ USE A STEAM FACIAL ON A WEEKLY BASIS TO HELP CLEANSE THE SKIN.

# Dry and sore lips

It is quite simple to make your own soothing cream for lips chapped by sun, wind, weather or illness. You can also apply a simple mixture of honey and rosewater as a salve for sore or chapped lips.

LAVENDER LIP BALM

Beeswax and cocoa butter are rich emollients; lavender oil is well known for its healing ability.

*INGREDIENTS*

   *5ml/1 tsp beeswax*
   *5ml/1 tsp cocoa butter*
   *5ml/1 tsp wheatgerm oil*
   *5ml/1 tsp almond oil*
   *3 drops lavender essential oil*

**1** Put all but the last ingredient, into a bowl and set over a pan of simmering water. Stir until melted.

**2** Remove from the heat and allow to cool for a few minutes before mixing in the lavender oil. Pour into a small jar and leave to set.

▾ BEESWAX HAS A HIGH MELTING POINT, SO BE PATIENT.

# Dry and oily skin

**Moisturizing cream prevents dryness of the skin, keeps wrinkles at bay and protects your skin from the weather. If you like, substitute pot marigolds for the elderflowers. Splash a little tonic on to your face first to feel refreshed.**

DRY SKIN MOISTURIZER

Elderflowers have a reputation for lightening dry skin. Store this face cream in the refrigerator. It keeps for several months.

*INGREDIENTS*

  *120ml/4fl oz/½ cup water*
  *10ml/2 tsps dried elderflowers*
  *30ml/2 tbsp emulsifying*
    *ointment*
  *5ml/1 tsp beeswax*
  *30ml/2 tbsp almond oil*
  *2.5ml/½ tsp borax*

**1** Boil the water and pour over the dried elderflowers in a jar. Leave to stand for 30 minutes then strain.

**2** Put the emulsifying ointment, beeswax and almond oil into one bowl and the elderflower infusion and borax into another. Set both over hot water and stir until the oils melt and the borax dissolves.

**3** Remove from the heat and pour the elderflower mixture into the oils. Stir gently until incorporated. Leave to cool, stirring at intervals. Pour into a jar before it sets.

## Elderflower skin tonic

This refreshing skin tonic can be made to suit your skin type and should be applied to your face direct from the refrigerator. It keeps for a few days, or can be frozen in small quantities and thawed as required.

*INGREDIENTS*

*10 dried elderflower heads*
*300ml/½ pint/1¼ cups still bottled water, boiled*
*15ml/1 tbsp either cider vinegar for normal skin, or witch hazel for slightly oily skin, or vodka for very oily skin*

**1** Strip the elderflowers from the stems and place in a bowl. Pour the boiling water over the flowers. Cover with a tea towel and leave for 20 minutes. Add either the cider vinegar, witch hazel or vodka, cover and leave overnight to infuse.

**2** Strain into a sterilized jar, cover and allow to cool. Store chilled.

### Mint and marigold moisturizer for oily skin

USE 25G/1OZ FRESH MINT LEAVES WITH 15G/½ OZ FRESH MARIGOLD PETALS AND 600ML/1 PINT/2½ CUPS BOILING WATER WITH 30ML/2 TBSP VODKA.

# growing and harvesting herbs

Unless you are a keen cook or an enthusiastic gardener, chances are that you won't have a designated area for herbs in your garden. If space is tight, experiment first with bought herbs to see what suits you and responds well to the ailments you are susceptible to. You can then decide which herbs it is worth allotting space to. The advantage of growing your own herbs is in having a ready year-round supply, and of knowing how they have been grown. Even if you don't have a garden, you can still grow herbs in containers on a balcony or patio, or even on a windowsill.

# Growing herbs for healing

**If you are new to growing herbs, take heart, they are not very difficult to grow and reward you over and over again for very little effort. The easiest way to start is to buy pot-grown herbs and plant them out.**

SOIL

On the whole, herbs are undemanding and easy to grow. A free-draining lightish soil will suit the majority. Many herbs prefer light, sandy soils, similar to that provided by their Mediterranean homeland, and most will not stand heavy clay soils or waterlogged conditions. You can lighten soil by digging in sand, grit and organic matter, or you could consider growing your herbs in containers. The rule tends to be: silvery, needle-like leaves or tough foliage require sunny, well-drained conditions; soft green leaves tolerate partial shade; golden-leaved herbs will need sun.

▼ HERBS OFFER GLORIOUS SCENTS AND ADD STUNNING COLOUR TO A GARDEN.

## Site

A sunny, sheltered position protected from bitter winds will suit many herbs best. Some will need winter protection and a few, such as basil, will not survive and will need replanting every year. Aloe vera must be treated as a houseplant in colder regions.

## Maintenance

Many herbs are prolific growers. Harvesting them helps to keep them under control, but do not be afraid to cut them back ruthlessly from time to time and root out those that are overpowering their neighbours. Herbs kept on a kitchen windowsill should be rotated with other container herbs to ensure that they do not become so bereft of foliage that they die.

## Weeding

Remove weeds regularly to prevent them from competing with your herbs for moisture and nutrients. A light mulch of compost, applied in spring or autumn, can help to keep the herbs at their best.

# Growing herbs in containers

**Herbs grow well in containers if you follow a few common-sense tips. Choose from a small pot, hanging basket, window box, old clay sink, large wooden tub or trough, old chimneystack or even an old barrel.**

Make sure your container can give the roots room to spread out and that it has holes in the base. Put a layer of broken shards of terracotta pots in the base, then add a layer of sand or grit before filling with potting compost (soil mix). Never use garden soil, no matter what condition it is in – it may harbour weeds, pests and diseases. Add water-retaining gel if you like, since this helps with watering later on.

Extra fertilizer must be added after two weeks, with subsequent weekly feeds throughout the summer growing season to ensure you get the best from your plant.

Water frequently during the growing season. During the winter months water just enough to avoid drying out completely.

▼ A GROUP OF HERBS PLANTED IN DECORATIVE CONTAINERS CAN MAKE AN ATTRACTIVE FEATURE IN THE GARDEN.

# A trough for winter colds

Most of the herbs used here keep their leaves through the winter. However it is best to harvest them while they are growing vigorously and dry them for later use since they do not have the same potency while dormant in the winter.

*You will need*

*trough*
*broken terracotta pots*
*gravel or horticultural grit*
*potting compost (soil mix)*
*watering can*

*Herbs – black peppermint, hyssop, horehound, sage, purple sage, golden sage, thyme*

▼ THIS TROUGH WILL KEEP YOU SUPPLIED WELL THROUGHOUT THE YEAR WITH HERBS FOR TEAS AND COUGH REMEDIES.

**1** Put a layer of broken terracotta at the bottom of the trough. Add a layer of gravel or horticultural grit. Almost fill with a good quality potting compost.

**2** Tap the plants out of their pots and plant, firming around each one with extra compost. Put the tallest plants at the back and the thymes at the front. Top up with extra compost as necessary and water the plants in well.

# Pots for headache remedies

**Fresh or dried herbs made into teas and compresses can help to relieve the tension brought on by headaches and migraines. Feverfew will relieve a migraine, but it is bitter, so eat the leaves sandwiched between bread slices.**

*You will need*

- *half-barrel with drainage holes*
- *heavy-duty black plastic*
- *staples*
- *broken terracotta pots*
- *horticultural grit*
- *soilless compost (growing medium)*
- *sharp sand*
- *watering can*

*Herbs – feverfew, lavender, St John's wort, marjoram, rosemary*

▼ Taking herbs as teas will help relieve the symptoms of a headache.

**1** Insert the plastic liner into the tub and staple it to the side, overlapping the plastic where necessary.

**2** Put in a layer of broken terracotta pots at the bottom, and top up with grit. Add soilless compost (growing medium), mixed with sand, to come a third of the way up the tub.

**3** Fill with a gritty, open-textured potting compost (growing medium). Arrange the herbs in the tub. Plant up and water in well.

# Pots for bites and bruises

The plants used here make good salves and ointments to counteract the effects of bites and bruises. If you are susceptible to bruising or live in areas infested with insects having herbs to hand will make life easier.

▲ HERBS WITH STRUCTURE MAKE STRIKING FEATURES IN POTS.

*YOU WILL NEED*

stone urn
broken terracotta pots
horticultural grit
loam-based potting compost
(soil mix) mixed in equal parts
with soilless potting compost
(growing medium)
trowel
watering can

*HERBS – aloe vera, comfrey, houseleek, pot marigold, yarrow*

1 Put a layer of broken terracotta pots in the base of the urn, then add a layer of grit.

2 Two-thirds fill the urn with the compost (soil mix).

3 Plant the aloe vera in the middle in its own pot so that it can be removed before the first frosts. Plant the yarrow and comfrey near the middle of the pot. Put the houseleeks around the outside, filling in with extra compost as necessary. Water the plants in well.

# Harvesting herbs

 **The best time to harvest the aerial parts of herbs is after their flower buds have formed but before they are in full bloom. Roots should be dug up in the autumn, cleaned and chopped into small pieces.**

Never pick herbs without being able to correctly identify them, or pick so many that you reduce next year's growth.

Spread the herbs out to dry in an airy position out of direct sunlight – an airing cupboard is an ideal place. Leafy bunches can be tied into little bundles and hung up. Spread flower heads on tissue or newspaper and dry them flat. It can take a week for them to dry.

1 Cut bunches of healthy material at mid-morning on a dry day.

2 Strip off the lower leaves, which may otherwise become damaged.

3 Bind the lower stems tightly with an elastic (rubber) band.

4 Gather as many bunches as you need, then hang them up to dry.

# Storing herbs

The volatile oils in herbs start to deteriorate quickly once the herbs are put in the light. Store dried herbs in separate, airtight containers away from the light and they will keep for up to six months.

Although many herbs retain an aromatic scent for several years, for medicinal purposes it is best to replace stocks every year since their potency declines with age.

▲ DRY INDIVIDUAL LEAVES ON A WIRE RACK, BEFORE STORING THEM.

▼ SOME HERBS CAN BE LAYERED IN SALT TO PRESERVE THEM. THIS ALSO FLAVOURS SALT.

▲ DARK BOTTLES MAKE GOOD STORAGE CONTAINERS FOR DRIED HERBS, OILS AND CREAMS.

Many shops stock dried herbs. Buy these only if they seem fresh – brightly coloured and strongly aromatic. Some herbal remedies are now available over the counter in the form of capsules, tablets or tinctures. Choose the simpler types that tell you exactly the type and quantity of herb involved.

## FREEZING HERBS

Instead of drying your herbs, you can store them in the freezer. This is especially useful for herbs such as parsley or lemon balm, which lose their flavour when dried.

# Herb directory

The herbs that follow are useful for common problems. Herbal remedies do not usually work instantly, so give them time to take effect. Seek the advice of a qualified practitioner if symptoms persist.

*Allium sativum,* GARLIC
This herb has many medicinal purposes. It helps to lower blood pressure and blood cholesterol, and is thought to inhibit blood clotting which leads to circulatory diseases. As a decongestant, garlic soothes coughs and colds and has strong antiseptic properties.

*Aloe vera,* ALOE VERA
The tall clusters of fleshy, spiny-toothed leaves that ooze a thick gel when opened. This plant contains anti-inflammatory agents, minerals, antioxidant vitamins C, E, B$_{12}$ and beta carotene. The gel from the leaves is applied to burns, bites, bruises and skin irritations.

*Anethum graveolens,* DILL
An aromatic annual, with a single stem and feathery leaves. Dill is a cooling, soothing herb. It aids digestion, and prevents constipation. Poultices of the leaves are applied to boils and to reduce swelling and joint pains. Seeds are chewed to cure bad breath.

*Borago officinalis,* BORAGE
This bristly plant with blue flowers flourishes in the wild. Borage is a cooling, anti-inflammatory herb with diuretic properties. Use infusions externally to treat inflamed skin, or as a mouthwash. The flowers can be taken as a tea to dispel depression and nervous anxiety.

*Calendula officinalis,* MARIGOLD
This yellowy-orange flower has many medicinal uses. As a tincture it can be used to treat burns, bites and stings; as an infusion, it refreshes the skin, as a mouthwash it relieves mouth ulcers.

*Chamaemelum nobile*, CHAMOMILE
A spreading plant with pretty flowers. Chamomile has antiseptic, anti-inflammatory properties and is soothing and sedative. Taken as a tea, it alleviates nausea and indigestion and helps promote sleep. In an ointment it soothes skin irritations and insect bites. As a steam inhalation it may ease asthma, sinusitis or catarrh.

*Echinacea purpurea*, CONEFLOWER
This hardy perennial has pinkish purple daisy-like flowers. The dried roots and rhizomes are made into capsules and powders to treat the common cold. Recent research has shown echinacea has a beneficial effect on the immune system. It can also be taken internally as a tea for kidney infections, or used externally as a compress for skin diseases, boils and abscesses.

*Filipendula ulmaria*, MEADOWSWEET
A plant of damp fields, meadowsweet has yellowy-white flowers with a distinctive sweet scent. Taken as a tea it helps reduce heartburn, and lessens acidity; it may help rheumatism, arthritis and urinary infections.

*Glycyrrhiza glabra*, LICORICE
The licorice plant produces ovate leaves, small flowers and long seed pods. It is the root of the plant that contains the active properties and has been used to treat stomach disorders, sore throats and respiratory infections. It has soothing, anti-inflammatory properties and is added to cough mixtures, lozenges and laxatives.

*Helianthus annuus*, SUNFLOWER
This annual is recognizable for its huge daisy-like yellow/orange flowerheads up to 30cm/1ft across and its central brown disc, filled with black and white seeds. Sunflower seeds are a good source of vitamin E which has antioxidant properties. They are high in polyunsaturates which promote cell maintenance and lower blood pressure.

*Hypericum perforatum,*
St John's wort
Small leaves and yellow flowers appear around the time of the summer solstice – it is now well known as an anti-depressant and can be taken as a tea or in tablet form. As a tincture it is used to soothe bites and stings.

*Hyssopus officinalis,*
Hyssop
An evergreen with dark green leaves and blue flowers borne in summer, hyssop will grow happily in a pot. Made into an infusion or a tea, it clears catarrh and sometimes reduces hayfever symptoms.

*Juniperus communis,*
Juniper
This hardy coniferous evergreen shrub has needle-like leaves and small spherical fruits that ripen to a black-blue colour. The berries have a sweet, pine-like flavour that explains their effectiveness in clearing nasal passages when used in a steam inhalant. The berries have antiseptic and anti-inflammatory properties and are thought to be useful for treating gout, arthritis and colic.

*Lavandula,* Lavender
This shrub has grey foliage and blue, white or pink flowers. Lavender oil eases muscle stiffness, soothes chapped skin and clears the nose. Taken in a tea, lavender relieves headaches, stress and nervous tension and promotes sleep.

*Marrubium vulgare,*
Horehound
Commonly known as white horehound, this is a downy perennial with white flowers that contain a bitter juice. Infusions of the fresh leaves are taken for coughs, colds and chest infections. Combined with antiseptic sage, hyssop or thyme it makes an effective throat gargle.

*Melissa officinalis,*
Lemon balm
The soft green leaves of this bushy perennial release a fresh lemony scent when crushed. Lemon balm has sedative relaxing, digestive properties. Infusions of the fresh leaves

are taken to ease nervous anxiety, depression, tension headaches and indigestion. It has insect-repellent properties, is anti-bacterial and when applied externally as poultices and ointments will help to heal sores, skin irritations, insect bites and stings.

*Mentha*, MINT
There are many varieties of mint and each has its own characteristics. Peppermint is taken as a tea for colds and to aid digestion. The essential oil has decongestant properties and can be used as an inhalant to relieve colds, chest infections, catarrh and asthma. It repels insects.

*Ocimum basilicum*, BASIL
This half-hardy annual grows to 60cm/2ft tall and has soft, ovate, bright green leaves. Basil has antidepressant, antiseptic, soothing properties and is best used fresh. Rub the leaves or dilute essential oil on to insect bites and stings, or make them into an infusion to treat colds. The leaves are made into cough syrups

with honey, and the essential oil can be used in a massage oil to treat depression and anxiety.

*Origanum*, MARJORAM
All varieties of marjoram have a warm, pungent scent, oval leaves and little clusters of pink, white or purple flowers. This herb has relaxing properties and is mildly antiseptic. It may be taken as a tea to relieve nervous anxiety, insomnia, headaches, colds, bronchial infections, indigestion, and painful periods. The essential oil is diluted to treat muscular aches, pains, sprains and stiff joints.

*Passiflora incarnata*, PASSIONFLOWER
This exotic-looking flower has subtropical origins and large creamy-white to lavender flowers with purple calyces. The whole plant is used for medicinal preparations, but used at home, the dried leaves can be taken in teas in combination with other herbs to relieve pain, especially headaches and to ease nervous conditions and insomnia.

*Petroselinum crispum*,
PARSLEY
This well-known frost-hardy perennial grows on a short taproot and produces three-pinnate leaves. Parsley is rich in vitamins A and E, and acts as an antioxidant. Parsley tea is sometimes used to treat coughs and jaundice, but it should not be used for self-medication.

*Rosa*, ROSE
Roses were once widely valued for their medicinal properties, but their main therapeutic use now is in aromatherapy. The essential oil is used to relieve depression and nervous anxiety. Roses are also used in natural beauty preparations to treat sensitive skins.

ROSEHIP
These are the berry-like fruits of the rose plant and are a rich source of vitamin C, hence their efficacy in teas taken to prevent or relieve colds and flu. Rosehips are used in cooking to make vinegars, syrups, preserves and wines.

*Rosmarinus officinalis*,
ROSEMARY
This herb has needle-shaped, grey-green leaves and pale blue flowers. It is a restorative herb with antiseptic and antibacterial properties. Taken as tea it helps reduce cold symptoms, fatigue and headaches. As a tincture it is taken to soothe nervous tension and depression. Used as a massage oil it will help ease rheumatism and muscular pain.

*Salvia*, SAGE
An evergreen shrub with downy, grey-green leaves and blue flowers. Sage is an antiseptic, anti-bacterial herb. Infusions of the leaves are used as a gargle or mouthwash for bad breath, sore throats, mouth ulcers, gum disease, laryngitis, and tonsillitis. The fresh leaves rubbed on teeth, will help cleanse them. Sage tea is a tonic that aids indigestion and menopausal problems. This herb can be used in combination with other herbs to treat a variety of symptoms. Made into a compress, its antiseptic properties will help to heal wounds.

*Sambucus nigra*, ELDERFLOWER
The hardy elder shrub grows freely in hedgerows. Used in facial tonics and moisturizers, it is good for the skin. Made into a tea, it helps coughs and colds as well as disturbed sleep.

 *Symphytum officinale*, COMFREY
A furry-leaved plant with blue or white flowers, comfrey grows in the wild. Historically it was known as a healing agent for fractures. Comfrey leaves are made into poultices, compresses and ointments and applied externally to bruises, varicose veins, inflamed muscles and to strained tendons.

 *Tanacetum parthenium*, FEVERFEW
With green foliage and white daisy-like flowers, feverfew is especially successful in treating migraine – two or three leaves should be eaten in a sandwich. Take care, however, since prolonged consumption of feverfew can cause mouth ulcers.

 *Thymus*, THYME
There are many varieties of thyme, but the one with acknowledged medicinal properties is *Thymus vulgaris* with white flowers. It makes a good mouthwash to combat mouth ulcers, and as a tea soothes coughs, colds and sore throat symptoms. Its essential oil eases tense muscles and a sachet of dried thyme can induce sleep.

 *Valeriana officinalis*, VALERIAN
Not to be confused with the red garden flower of the same name, valerian is a perennial with white flowers. It is best known for its sedative qualities and for its ability to act as a stress-buster.

 *Zingiber officinale*, GINGER
The root of the ginger plant is used in herbal remedies. Ginger has its own distinct spicy smell and warming qualities. It is a stimulant that encourages sweating to eliminate toxins and dispel catarrh, hence its use in cold remedies.

# Index